Consultants

Timothy Rasinski, Ph.D.
Kent State University

Lori Oczkus, M.A.
Literacy Consultant

This book was originally reviewed by Sally Ride Science and Jane Weir, MPhys.

Publishing Credits

Rachelle Cracchiolo, M.S.Ed., *Publisher*
Conni Medina, M.A.Ed., *Managing Editor*
Dona Herweck Rice, *Series Developer*
Emily R. Smith, M.A.Ed., *Content Director*
Stephanie Bernard/Susan Daddis, M.A.Ed., *Editors*
Robin Erickson, *Senior Graphic Designer*

The TIME logo is a registered trademark of TIME Inc. Used under license.

Image Credits: Cover and p. 1 (front) Colorized by Dana Keller, (back) Science Source; pp. 4–5 Adrian Grycuk; p. 6 Akademie/Alamy Stock Photo; p. 7 (front) The Print Collector/Alamy Stock Photo, (back) Sarin Images/Granger, NYC; pp. 8, 9 Granger, NYC; p. 11 Emmanuel Lansyer/Getty Images; p. 12 Wellcome Library, London; p. 13 The Print Collector/Alamy Stock Photo; p. 14, 20–21 Science Source; p. 15 Voisin/Phanie/Science Source; p. 16 Astrid & Hanns-Frieder Michler/Science Source; p. 17 Jacques Boyer/Roger Viollet/Getty Images; p. 18 AFP/Getty Images; p. 19 (top) American Philosophical Society, (bottom) Yale College class of 1874 class album. Manuscripts & Archives, Yale University; [. 20 AIP/Science Source; p. 22 SPL/Science Source; p. 23 (top) © Daily Herald Archive/National Media Museum/Science & Society Picture Library , (bottom) INTERFOTO/Alamy Stock Photo; pp. 24–25 Apic/Getty Images; p. 26 Georgios Kollidas/Alamy Stock Photo; p. 29 Mary Evans Picture Library/Science Source; all other images from iStock and/or Shutterstock.

Teacher Created Materials

5301 Oceanus Drive
Huntington Beach, CA 92649-1030
http://www.tcmpub.com

ISBN 978-1-4258-5159-0

© 2017 Teacher Created Materials, Inc.

Table of Contents

Radioactive! 4
The Girl from Poland 8
Discovering Radium 14
Bringing Her Work to the World 24
The Final Years 26
Glossary 28
Index 29
Check It Out! 30
Try It! 31
About the Authors 32

Radioactive!

It's like something out of a science fiction movie. Her papers are kept in lead-lined containers. If you receive permission to study them firsthand, you must wear protective clothing. The fact is, the documents are highly **radioactive**. Exposure to them can be sickening—even deadly. Those who want to study the vast amount of paperwork left behind by the great twentieth century scientist, Marie Curie, must take great care not to follow her poisoned path to the grave.

The truth is, Curie is one of the most brilliant, important, and revolutionary scientists the world has ever known. She transformed the way people look at the world of energy and the resources available to us. But in doing so, she paid the ultimate price. She worked daily with radioactive materials, long before anyone knew their dangers. She took detailed notes of her observations and experiments, as a good scientist does. Little did she know, her painstaking work was slowly killing her.

Radioactivity

When something gives off energy, it produces **radiation.** For example, the sun radiates heat and light. Curie did not think *radiation* was the right word to describe the energy coming from substances she studied. She called it *radioactivity*. It is **generated** when the nuclei within the **atoms** of radioactive substances break down.

Marie Curie Museum in Warsaw, Poland

1,500 Years

Many people think that the materials Curie left behind will stay radioactive for the next 1,500 years. These include her notebooks, clothing, and furniture. People who are allowed access to her notebooks must sign a **liability waiver**.

An Important Scientist

Marie Curie spent her life studying energy called *radiation*. In fact, she invented the word *radioactive* to describe this energy. Her investigations and experiments helped other scientists understand how atoms work. Curie also learned many things that became **instrumental** in finding new ways to treat **cancer**.

Curie was the first woman to win the world's highest award for science, the **Nobel Prize**, in 1903. Her work was so successful that she won a second Nobel Prize in 1911. Her husband, Pierre, with whom she won the first prize, was also a scientist of note. The two worked together until his untimely death. Their daughter Irène grew up to become a famous scientist and she, too, won a Nobel Prize. Irène's two children are also important scientists. They have continued the family legacy of scientific inquiry.

From her earliest days, Curie was known as a determined and focused worker and a brilliant scientist. She would not stop investigating until she found answers to her questions. Her work with radiation was also dangerous. She died from aplastic anemia, a cancer of the blood. It was caused by working with radioactive materials.

The Nobel Prize

The Nobel Prize was first awarded in 1901. It is given to men and women for their work in science, writing, medicine, economics, and efforts to bring peace to the world. The award includes a medal, a diploma, and money that can be used to continue the work.

"Fairy Lights"

The Curies kept radioactive **elements** such as **uranium** and **plutonium** in their home, and Pierre even carried them in his pockets. Curie thought the glow that **radium** gave off was pretty and magical, so she kept a sample on her nightstand to use as a nightlight. She wrote that it looked like "faint, fairy lights."

Pierre Curie

The Girl from Poland

Curie was born Maria Sklodowska in Poland, on November 7, 1867, the youngest of five children. Her father was a high school science teacher, and her mother was the principal of a private school for girls.

Curie was always a very good student, and she especially enjoyed studying science and language arts. She graduated from high school at age 15, but she wanted to keep learning. Unfortunately, at that time, Polish girls were not allowed to attend college.

Curie and her older sister, Bronislawa (called Bronia), started studying at a secret school. Professors taught classes in private homes. The sisters soaked up all the knowledge they could. Then, they made plans to travel to Paris, France, where girls were allowed to go to college. Bronia left first and studied to become a doctor. Curie stayed in Poland, working as a teacher to send money to Bronia. Finally, it was her turn. In 1891, she took the train to Paris and joined Bronia.

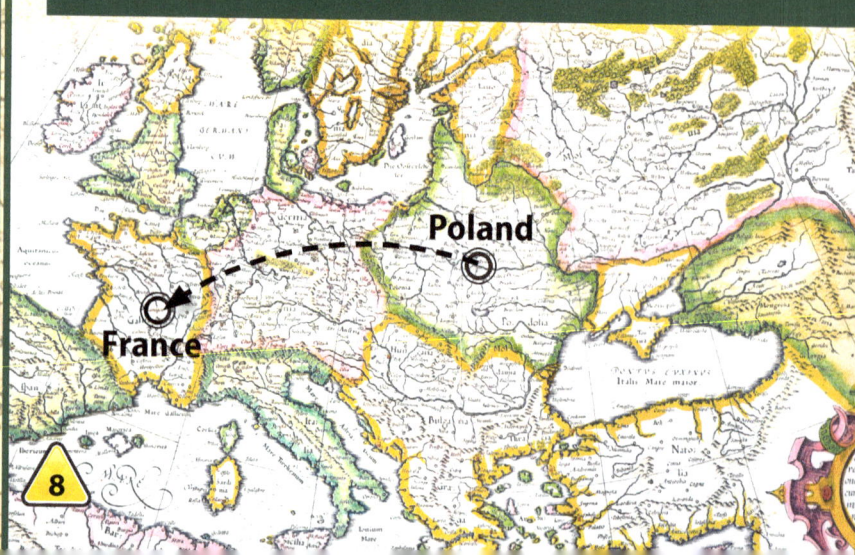

Here is Curie (far left) with her father and sisters. Her mother died when she was just 11 years old.

Free to Study

In the late 1800s, it was hard for anyone to study in Poland, let alone girls. This was because the Russian government ruled Poland and wanted everyone to speak and study only Russian subjects. Curie had to leave home to continue her education. France was one place where she could enjoy this freedom.

THINK LINK

- Why is it important that people sign a liability waiver to have access to Curie's notebooks?
- Would Curie have studied radioactivity if she knew the risks of the work?
- Historically, and even today, there are fewer opportunities for women around the world to be educated than there are for men. Why is that?

Studying in Paris

Curie studied at the University of Paris, also called the Sorbonne. While there, she lived alone in a small, drafty attic. Education was very important to her and worth the discomfort and loneliness.

Curie loved her science classes, where she enjoyed and excelled in **chemistry** and **physics** but had ongoing trouble with mathematics. To learn the challenging subject, she hired a tutor and worked many extra hours, studying late nearly every night. Her education was worth it.

All Curie's classes were taught in French, but Curie only spoke, read, and wrote Polish. The only way to succeed was to learn to read, write, and speak French—which is exactly what she did.

Curie didn't let anything stop her from doing her schoolwork; in fact, sometimes she even forgot to eat! In the end, she finished her studies in 1893 at the top of her class, ranking first in physics. She also won a scholarship for further study of mathematics. Despite her earlier troubles, she finished second in her math class in 1894.

Hunger

Curie was a very poor student. Sometimes she would be so busy that she would forget to eat. However, there were also times when she would faint from hunger because she simply could not afford food. She often lived on bread and tea.

Sorbonne

The Sorbonne is one of Europe's oldest universities, dating back to AD 1150. It was named for Robert de Sorbon, a French **theologian** in the thirteenth century.

The courtyard of the old Sorbonne in 1886.

Marie and Pierre

In 1893, Curie was recognized for her scientific skill and offered a job studying magnets and how they interact with different kinds of steel. In January 1894, while searching for lab space, she met a shy introvert named Pierre Curie. He was a professor at the School of Physics at the Sorbonne and the head of the physics laboratory. Pierre Curie was already famous for his work with magnets and crystals. After working closely together in the lab, Marie and Pierre developed a romantic relationship. The two married just one year after meeting. Marie wore a dark blue outfit to the wedding—the same outfit she wore in the lab. Soon, the young couple had two daughters, Irène and Ève.

At the time, society made it difficult for women scientists to work alone, and so many women like Curie married fellow scientists. The Curies worked together for many years.

Note Taker

Curie carefully recorded notes about all her experiments in hundreds of laboratory notebooks. She also kept detailed personal notations. Among the scientific information, she included memos on things such as a jelly recipe and how much it cost to do her laundry.

A Modern Family

Curie was a very practical, organized woman. She was determined to be a good scientist, and also a good wife and mother. It was very important to both her and her husband that they continue their work together. So they hired a servant to work around the house and asked Pierre's father to babysit their children.

Pierre and Marie Curie out for a bicycle ride

Discovering Radium

Curie needed a subject to research and study for her doctorate, the highest degree a person can earn. She was especially interested in studying the work of two scientists who worked with rays of energy. One had discovered X-rays. The other found that the element uranium also gives off energy.

Curie suspected that the energy from uranium had to do with its atoms. Atoms are the basic building blocks that make up everything in the universe. Curie and her husband tested other elements to see if they **generated** radiation. Through this process, they discovered a new element, which Curie named polonium after her home country of Poland. She also made up the word *radioactive* to describe substances that create radiation.

Labs Then

Curie's laboratory was an old shack with a leaky roof, in which medical students used to **dissect cadavers**. It was impossible to control the conditions in the lab. Curie sweltered in the summer and froze in the winter. Modern scientists can't imagine how she managed to find the atomic weight of radium under such conditions.

Still, the Curies had more to discover. Their work led them to discover another element, which they named *radium*. It took many years to prove their findings. They had to find a way to isolate the substances in their pure forms. They also had to find the **atomic weight** of each element, which is the weight of just one of its atoms.

Labs Now

Modern labs are clean and comfortable with fully controlled conditions. The Institut Curie in Paris is named after Curie. It offers some of the best lab conditions in the world. Researchers are able to adapt or maintain conditions to the needs of their experiments.

The First Nobel Prize

The Curies were determined to prove they had discovered new elements. First, they worked to find pure radium. They found a large lab and a huge amount of pitchblende, a brownish-black mineral that contains radium. At the same time, Curie finished her doctorate, wrote reports, and taught at a women's college. The Curies taught a great deal to earn money to support their research.

In 1902, the Curies successfully isolated radium and found its atomic weight. They believed their discovery belonged to the world, so they shared the details with other scientists. They did not seek a **patent** and shared their work for free.

Wonder Woman!

The Curies bought tons of pitchblende in 50-pound (22.68 kilogram) bags. Curie carried nearly 40 of these bags, dumped them into pots, and added acid and a large amount of water. Then, she stirred the mixture with a long metal rod to dissolve the pitchblende. The metal rod was nearly as tall as she was! She did all this work to make one-tenth of a **gram** of radium.

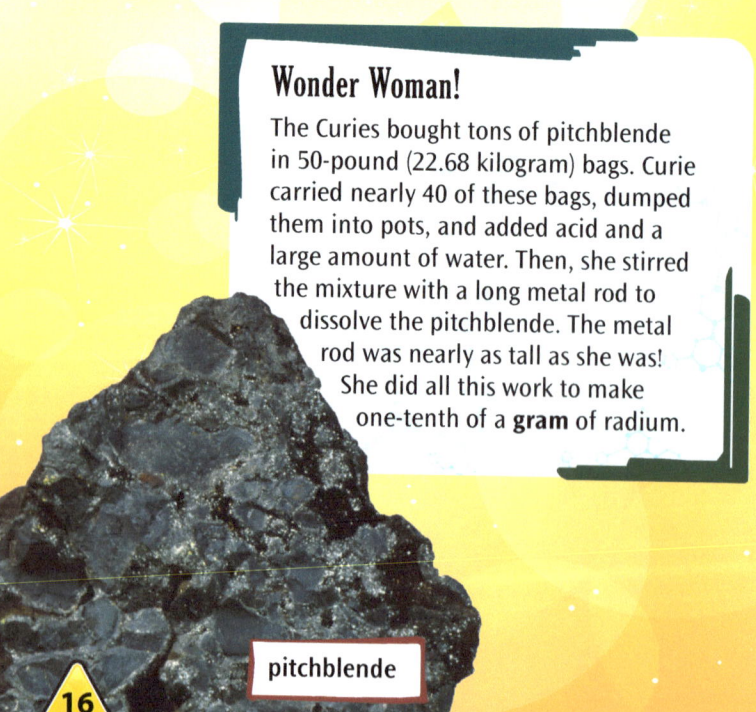

pitchblende

During this time, both scientists found themselves tired and losing weight. Their fingers were numb and burned. Perhaps they didn't realize that these symptoms were a result of handling radium. Some experts think the Curies knew radium would make them sick, but they ignored the dangers to continue their work.

In 1903, the world recognized the Curies' work with radiation by awarding them the Nobel Prize in Physics. At first, the award was to be given to Pierre and another scientist, Henri Becquerel, for his work with radioactivity. Pierre refused the award unless Marie was included. The Nobel organization finally agreed. But by that time, the Curies were too sick to travel to accept their award in person.

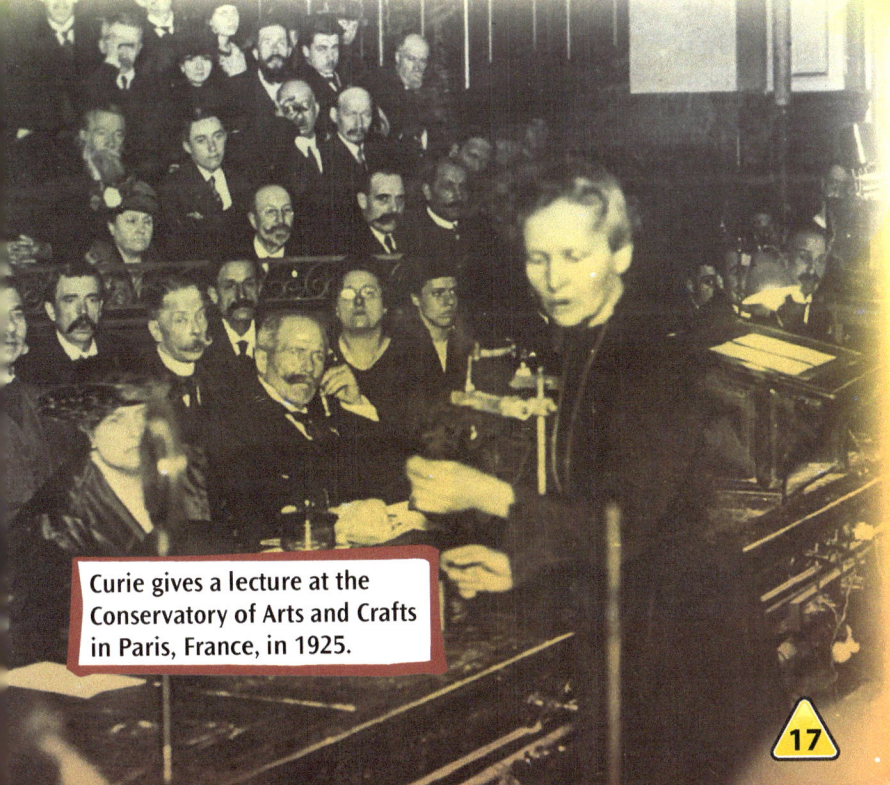

Curie gives a lecture at the Conservatory of Arts and Crafts in Paris, France, in 1925.

On Her Own

On a rainy day in April 1906, Pierre Curie rushed through the streets of Paris on his way to a meeting. He stumbled into the path of a horse-drawn wagon. Sadly, he was killed.

Marie Curie was left to raise their daughters and continue to research on her own. At the time, it was almost unheard of for a woman scientist to work alone.

Remarkably, Curie was asked to replace her husband as Professor of General Physics at the Sorbonne and to head the physics laboratory there. She accepted, becoming the first woman to hold either post in the 650-year history of the school.

Curie began to plan the Radium Institute to continue her work. She studied how to use radium to treat disease and researched to find an exact unit of measure for radiation. She found it, and it is now called the **curie unit**.

Marie Curie with her two daughters, Ève and Irène in 1908

Support for Female Scientists

Another female scientist, Myrtle Hildred Blewett, was born in 1911 and lived for 93 years, studying physics all her life. In 2005, a scholarship in her name was first awarded. Blewett had struggled in her career due to lack of funds and hindrances because she was a woman. She didn't want other women in science to struggle. Her scholarship is meant for women returning to physics after caring for their families.

Breaking Barriers

African Americans in science have often had struggles similar to women in science, and at one time, few received any education at all. In 1878, Edward Alexander Bouchet became the first African American to earn a doctorate degree in science. He was the sixth American of any race to earn such a degree in physics. But black men in his time were not supported in physics, and universities would not accept him as a professor. He spent his career teaching and studying in high schools with poor labs.

The Second Nobel Prize

Radium was accepted as a new element and was used around the world to treat cancer. It's ironic that this element was used to treat cancer, but it also caused cancer. In the wake of Pierre's death, Curie continued to search for an even purer form of radium. She succeeded and found a more accurate atomic weight for radium, too.

Her illness progressed from all the years she handled radium. Though she was very sick, she continued to work even when some people began to question her ability. She kept details of her work and daily life in her notebooks. She also studied the work of other scientists in the field.

The Langevin Link

After Pierre's death, Curie had a lengthy relationship with Paul Langevin. He was one of her husband's former students. Many years later, Curie's granddaughter, Hélène, married Langevin's grandson, Michael.

Einstein and Curie

In 1911, Curie was awarded a second Nobel Prize, this time for chemistry. It was for the discovery of radium and polonium. But once again, she almost did not attend the ceremony. It had come to light that she'd had a relationship with a married man. The newspapers referred to Curie as a "homewrecker," and she was threatened by angry crowds. Acclaimed scientist Albert Einstein reached out to Curie to encourage her. He expressed deep admiration for her and her work. Curie attended the ceremony, and eventually the fervor died down.

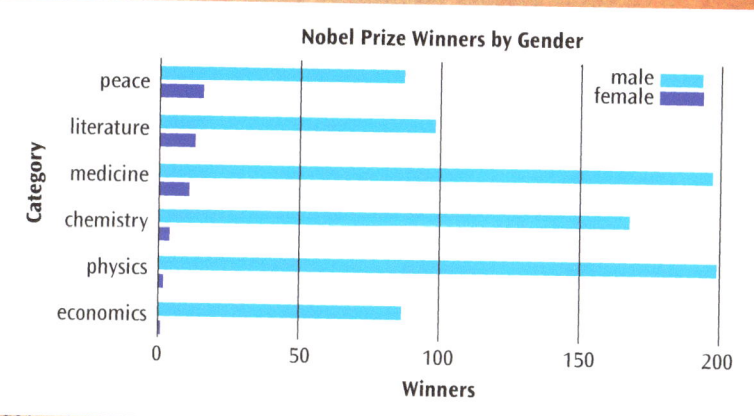

STOP! THINK...

- What might account for the enormous disparity between male and female winners of the Nobel Prize?
- Women have more awards for peace and literature than for the sciences or economics. Are there any historic reasons why that is so?
- What might it take to shift the balance of winners to be more equal?

Radium Craze

People in the early 1900s loved radium! They drank it to cure stomach cancer. They used it to make the faces of watches and airplane instruments glow in the dark. They put it in makeup so that it sparkled.

Factory workers who painted watch dials with radium were called Radium Girls, and they enjoyed the trendy products as much as anyone. Believing the radium paint was harmless, they had fun painting their fingernails and teeth with the substance. But over time, they began to notice strange things. For example, when they blew their noses, their handkerchiefs glowed in the dark. Then, the workers began to lose their teeth. Eventually, they died of cancer.

Too Much!

Because of its popularity as well as its use in treating cancer, the price of one gram of radium inflated to $100,000. This figure was beyond Curie's reach! She had discovered it, but she could no longer afford it.

Five of the Radium Girls sued their employers. It came to light that scientists working with radium used protection, but the employees were not cautioned or protected. The lawsuit proved to be difficult, but the Radium Girls eventually received a cash settlement. Laws protecting employees from workplace diseases were put into place because of the **litigation**. Eventually, people stopped using radium in everyday products.

radium watches and clocks from the early 1900s

Bringing Her Work to the World

It was important to Curie that the world would benefit from her work. She spent her last years making sure that happened.

World War I

Curie knew that x-rays would be useful in treating wounded soldiers. Doctors could see where bones were broken or bullets lodged. So Curie and her daughter Irène worked to get x-ray services to the front lines. They trained 150 women volunteers to take x-rays, established more than 200 x-ray rooms, and raised funds to buy x-ray equipment. Curie and her team took one million x-rays during World War I. If there was no one to help load and ship the equipment to the military hospitals, Curie did it herself.

Curie is surrounded by her students, other physicists, and members of the U.S. task force in 1919.

A Gift

In 1915, Curie returned to studying radium, which was by then being used all over the world to treat cancer. Radium had made Curie very famous—but it had also grown outrageously expensive. Curie only owned one gram of radium, which she had snuck out of Paris during the war. But to continue her research, she needed more.

Luckily, Curie had many admirers in the United States, and 10 wealthy American women raised more than $100,000 to buy one more gram of radium for Curie. In 1921, Curie made the long and difficult journey to America to accept this gift. Her health was very poor. The radiation sickness was getting worse.

Where There's a Will

When the German army was about to invade Paris, Curie had to protect her supply of radium, which she needed to continue her work. She packed the radioactive substance in a heavy lead case. Although she could barely lift the case, she carried it on board a train and escaped with the radium intact.

Unknown Energy

Curie's work with radioactivity led future scientists to study the inner workings of atoms. Before her discoveries, most scientists thought that atoms could not be changed. Further research proved there was energy inside atoms that could be released by explosions.

The Final Years

Curie returned home with her gift of radium, but she grew weaker and weaker from radiation sickness. Her eyesight was threatened, and finally, she became ill with cancer. In 1934, Curie died of the disease. The world mourned the loss of this great scientist.

But Curie had left a remarkable legacy. Her work led to many important findings, including the use of radiation to treat cancer, kill organisms that spoil food, find weaknesses in bridges, find smoke in homes, and even determined the age of dinosaur bones.

Because of Curie, there is also a new branch of science: the study of radioactivity. Her discovery of radium and its uses changed the way people think about matter and energy. Scientists continue to build on her work.

Curie was afraid her discoveries would be used to make weapons, and her fears were realized when the atomic bomb was made. But her work has also done great good in the world—and that's exactly what she hoped to do.

Scientific Legacy

In 1935, Irène Joliot-Curie and her husband, Frederic Joliot, won the Nobel Prize in Chemistry. The award was in recognition of their work in artificial radioactivity.

Surrounded by Radiation

Not all radiation is as strong and dangerous as the energy from the radium handled by the Curies. In fact, without the sun's radiation, there would be no life on Earth. Staying in the sun for hours and hours can be too much of a good thing, though. Not only can you get sunburned, but you can also face long-term skin damage.

Glossary

atomic weight—the amount of matter contained in a single atom

atoms—the smallest particles of an element

cadavers—dead bodies, especially ones to be dissected for medical study

cancer—a disease in which groups of cells form tumors and spread throughout the body

chemistry—a branch of science that studies the structure of substances and how they combine and change under different conditions

curie unit—the exact unit of measure for radiation

dissect—to cut open and apart for purposes of scientific investigation

elements—nature's basic substances made up of a single kind of atom

generated—started, grew

gram—a metric unit of mass

instrumental—crucial in helping something happen

liability waiver—release of another party's responsibility in a person's own well-being

litigation—legal action

Nobel Prize—a prize awarded each year for work in the fields of chemistry, physics, medicine, economics, peace, and literature

patent—legal ownership of an invention so that the holder is the only one who can sell it

physics—the study of matter, energy, force, and motion

plutonium—a radioactive element used to make nuclear weapons

radiation—the process of giving off energy

radioactive—giving off energy as a substance's atomic nuclei break apart

radium—a radioactive element

theologian—someone who studies religion

uranium—a radioactive element found in pitchblende and used in nuclear power stations

Index

atom, 5–6, 14–15
atomic bomb, 26
atomic weight, 15–16, 20
Becquerel, Henri, 17
Blewett, Myrtle, 19
Bouchet, Edward, 19
cancer, 6, 20, 22, 25–26
chemistry, 10, 21
Curie, Ève, 12
Curie, Irène, 6, 12, 24
Curie, Pierre, 6–7, 12–13, 17, 18, 20
curie unit, 18
doctorate, 14, 16, 19
Einstein, Albert, 21
element, 7, 14–16, 20
energy, 4–6, 14, 26–27
eyesight, 26
France, 8–9
Institut Curie, 15
laboratory, 12, 14, 16, 18
Langevin, Paul, 20
Nobel Prize, 6, 17, 20–21
physics, 10, 12, 17–19
pitchblende, 16
Poland, 8–9, 14
polonium, 14, 21
radiation, 5–6, 14, 18, 25–27
radioactivity, 5–6, 17, 26
radium, 7, 14–16, 18, 20–23, 25–27
Radium Girls, 22–23
Radium Institute, 18, 25
Russia, 9
Sklodowska, Bronia, 8
Sklodowska, Maria, 8
Sorbonne, 10–12, 18
United States, 25
University of Paris, 10
uranium, 7, 14
World War I, 24–25
X-rays, 14, 24

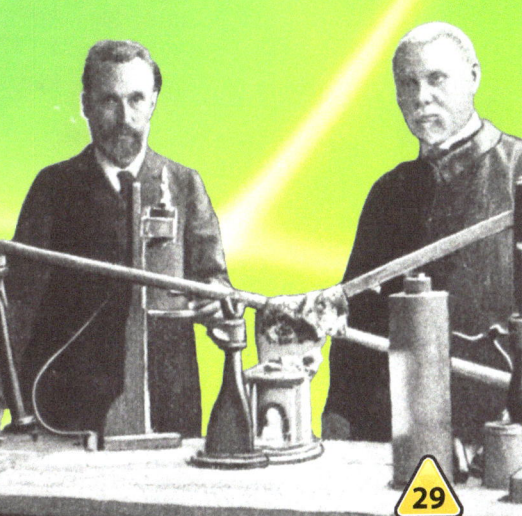

Check It Out!

Books

Atkins, Jeannine. 2010. *Borrowed Names*. Henry Holt & Co.

Curie, Ève. 2001. *Madam Curie: A Biography*. Da Capo Press.

DK editors. 2008. *DK Biography: Marie Curie*. DK Children.

Gregory, D.W. 2003. *Radium Girls*. Dramatic Publishing Company.

Poulsen, David A. 2016. *And Then the Sky Exploded*. Dundurn.

Videos

Bradshaw, Gideon. 2013. *The Genius of Marie Curie: The Woman Who Lit up the World*. British Broadcasting Channel.

LeRoy, Mervyn. 1943. *Madame Curie*. Metro-Goldwyn-Mayer.

PBS. 2015. *The Mystery of Matter: Marie Curie: The Radium Craze*.

Websites

The Nobel Foundation. *The Official Website of the Nobel Prize*. http://www.nobelprize.org.

Try It!

Marie Curie is the only woman to have won two Nobel Prizes—first in physics and then in chemistry. Now, it's your turn. You've been notified that you've won a Nobel Prize. Write a 200-word acceptance speech.

- Which Nobel Prize will you be awarded? Choose from the following categories: peace, literature, medicine, chemistry, physics, or economics.

- How is your work going to help or influence other people?

- Acknowledge any person who might have helped you, and include how he or she provided guidance.

- Write your speech and practice reciting it aloud.

- Work up the courage to present it to a real audience if one is available.

About the Authors

Elizabeth R. Cregan is a freelance writer living in Jamestown, Rhode Island. She enjoys writing about a wide variety of topics for children and young adults, including science, natural history, current events, and biography. She is also the owner of Cregan Associates, a consulting firm specializing in grant and technical writing for state government health and human services information technology clients.

Dona Herweck Rice has written hundreds of books, stories, and poems for kids on all kinds of topics, from pirates to heroes to why people have bad breath! Writing is her passion, but she also loves reading, live theater, dancing anytime and anywhere, and singing at the top of her lungs (although she'd be the first to tell you that this is not really a pleasure for anyone else). Dona was a teacher and is an acting coach. She lives in Southern California with her husband, two sons, and a cute but very silly little dog.

www.ingramcontent.com/pod-product-compliance
Lightning Source LLC
Chambersburg PA
CBHW042059290426
44113CB00001B/18